The Simple Cornbread Cookbook

Incredible and Unique Recipes for Your Favorite Cornbread

By: Owen Davis

Copyright © 2022 by Owen Davis.

Copyright Notice!

Please don't reproduce this book, guys! My team and I have worked long and hard to get the best quality content out there (this book!), and now that we have, we'd like to take care of it—but we need your help to do it. That means you aren't allowed to make any print or electronic reproductions, sell, re-publish, or distribute this book in parts or as a whole unless you have express written consent from me or my team.

While we have gone to great lengths to make sure the information presented is clear and precise, I nor any part of my team can be held liable for any damages or accidents that occur from any interpretations of this book. If you are unsure how to carry out certain steps from our recipes, look up videos or tutorials online to get a better understanding of how to do something. Remember that being in the kitchen always comes with certain risks, so take things easy and stay safe!

Table of Contents

Introduction 6

Chapter 1 Recipes 8

   1. Mom's Apple Cornbread Stuffing 9

   2. Oyster and Cornbread Dressing 11

   3. Quick Cornbread Dressing 14

   4. Rhubarb Cornbread Stuffing 16

   5. Italian Sausage and Cornbread Dressing 18

   6. Pork Sausage and Cornbread Stuffing 21

   7. Mushroom and Sausage Corn Bread Dressing 23

   8. Chestnut, Apple and Sausage Corn Bread Dressing 26

   9. Apple, Bacon, Sausage, And Cornbread Stuffing 29

   10. Savory Corn Bread Dressing 32

   11. Shrimp Corn Bread Dressing 34

   12. Southern Cornbread Dressing 37

   13. Southern Oyster Cornbread Dressing 40

   14. Spicy Cranberry and Pecan Cornbread Stuffing 42

   15. Ultimate Cornbread Stuffing 45

16. Minute Microwave Cornbread 48

17. Absolute Mexican Cornbread 50

18. Amusement Park Cornbread 52

19. Appalachian Corn Bread 54

20. Applesauce Cornbread 57

21. Authentic Mexican Corn Bread 59

22. Avocado Cheese Cornbread 61

23. Bacon Cornbread 63

24. Bacon Sweet Potato Cornbread 65

25. Baked Bean Cornbread 67

26. Banana Cornbread 69

27. Banana and Nut Cornbread 71

28. Barbecued Cornbread Muffins 73

29. Basic Buttermilk Cornbread 75

30. Basic Cornbread Muffins 77

31. Roasted Peppers and Monterey Jack Cornbread 79

32. Batter Cornbread 82

33. Blueberry Cornbread Muffins 84

34. The Best Cornbread Muffins 86

Conclusion 88

About the Author 89

Appendices 90

Introduction

Eating freshly baked bread at home makes us appreciate the value of high-quality ingredients.

Experienced bakers prefer baking bread over other cooking methods, and it's not easy to make, which causes beginners anxiety.

To bake successfully, you must have high-quality ingredients, the proper equipment, a balanced recipe, skilled hands, and creativity.

There are a variety of ways to prepare cornbread.

The best method is according to your preferences and the recipe you select. Some people prefer cornbread baked in an oven, while others prefer it cooked in a skillet.

This bread is typically made from cornmeal, rye flour, and spices. Cornbread is a generic term for various quick slices of bread, including gingerbread.

It's generally paired with hush puppies, chili, and soup.

Compared to other more challenging dishes, this cornbread recipe is simple to make.

When served at parties and gatherings, it adds delight and fun.

Let's get this party started!

Chapter 1 Recipes

1. Mom's Apple Cornbread Stuffing

"A quick recipe is end-all be-all stuffing."

Serving: 16

Preparation Time: 15 minutes

Ingredients

- 6 large Granny Smith apples, peeled and chopped
- 1 package (14 oz.) crushed cornbread stuffing
- 1/2 cup butter, melted
- 1 can (14½ oz.) chicken broth

Direction

Preheat the oven to 350°. Combine the liquefied butter, stuffing, and apples in a mixing bowl.

Mix in the broth thoroughly.

Add in a 13x9-inch oiled baking plate. Starts to bake for 35–40 minutes or until golden brown.

2. Oyster and Cornbread Dressing

"A fantastic dressing! To make it moister, add more chicken broth."

Serving: 12

Preparation Time: 45 minutes

Ingredients

- 2 (8 oz.) cans oysters, liquid reserved
- 3 tbsps. butter
- 1/2 cup chopped onions
- 1 (14.5 oz.) can of chicken broth
- 1/2 cup diced celery
- 1 tbsp. poultry seasoning
- 2 eggs
- 1/2 tsp. ground black pepper
- 2 (8 oz.) packages corn bread mix
- 1 1/2 tsp. dried sage

Direction

Prepare cornbread according to package directions.

Add the cornbread and crumble it in a large mixing bowl.

Preheat an oven to 175°C/350°F. Lightly grease a 9x9-inch baking pan.

Melt the butter in a large saucepan over medium-low heat.

Combine the parsley and onions.

Cook and occasionally stir until the onions are soft.

Place the mixture in a bowl with the breadcrumbs.

Chop the oysters, and combine the cornbread mixture.

Mix the oyster liquid, chicken broth, sage, poultry seasoning, pepper, eggs, and oysters.

Place in a baking dish.

In a preheated oven, bake for 45 minutes, uncovered.

3. Quick Cornbread Dressing

"This dish evolved from an altered casserole recipe into a stuffing side dish that goes well with chicken or pork."

Serving: 4-6

Preparation Time: 10 minutes

Ingredients

- 1 celery rib, finely chopped
- 1 tbsp. spicy brown mustard
- 1 package (8 oz.) of cornbread stuffing cubes
- 1 medium onion, finely chopped
- 1 cup water
- 1 can (8¼ oz.) cream-style corn
- 1 tbsp. butter, melted

Direction

Preheat the oven to 375°F.

Combine the onion, stuffing, water, and corn in a large mixing bowl.

Grease an 8-inch square baking dish with cooking spray.

Using a spoon, transfer the mixture to the baking dish.

Combine the mustard and butter and sprinkle over the stuffing.

Allow it to bake for 20 minutes without a cover in the oven.

4. Rhubarb Cornbread Stuffing

"This stuffing complements turkey, chicken, and ham.

It will leave your guests wanting for more."

Serving: 6-8

Preparation Time: 20 minutes

Ingredients

- 3 cups crushed cornbread stuffing
- 1/2 cup chopped walnuts
- 1/2 cup butter, divided
- 1 medium onion, chopped
- 1/2 cup sugar
- 5 cups chopped fresh or frozen rhubarb (1/2-inch pieces), thawed

Direction

Combine the rhubarb and sugar in a large mixing bowl. Set it aside.

Melt 2 tablespoons of butter in a large skillet and cook the onion until tender.

Then stir in the walnuts and the stuffing into the rhubarb mixture.

Warm the remaining butter in a small saucepan over medium heat before gently stirring it into the stuffing mixture.

Place in a greased 2-quart shallow roasting pan and bake at 325°F for 40 to 45 minutes, until the stuffing is thoroughly cooked and the top is light brown.

Serve while still warm.

5. Italian Sausage and Cornbread Dressing

"Add some sausage and some steak sauce to this cornbread dressing."

Serving: 12

Preparation Time: 30 minutes

Ingredients

- 1 package (19½ oz.) Italian turkey sausage links, casings removed
- 4 chopped medium onions (Use about 3 cups)
- 6 cups of cubes of French bread or day-old white bread
- 1/2 cup celery, chopped
- 2 large eggs
- 6 cups cornbread, coarsely crumbled
- 2 tbsps. steak sauce
- 2 tsp. onion salt
- 2 tsp. poultry seasoning
- 2 tsp. dried parsley flakes
- 1 tsp. garlic powder
- 1 tsp. baking powder
- 2½ to 3 cups of low-sodium chicken broth

Direction

Preheat the oven to 350°.

Cook the sausage in a 6-quart stockpot over medium-high heat for 6 to 8 minutes or until thoroughly cooked, chopping it up into crumbles

Remove with a slotted spoon, leaving the drippings in the pot.

Cook the celery and onions in drippings for 6 to 8 minutes or until soft.

Remove from heat and stir in sausage.

Toss the cornbread and cubed bread together.

Mix the baking powder, seasonings, steak sauce, and eggs in a small mixing bowl. Stir into the bread mixture.

Add enough broth to achieve the desired moistness.

Place in a well-oiled 3-quart or 13x9-inch baking dish.

Allow it to bake for 40 to 50 minutes or until lightly browned.

6. Pork Sausage and Cornbread Stuffing

"A stuffing mix side dish with jarred mushrooms and pork sausage."

Serving: 8

Preparation Time: 5 minutes

Ingredients

- 1 lb. bulk pork sausage
- 3½ cups of water
- 1 jar (7 oz.) of sliced mushrooms, drained
- 2 packages (6 oz. each) of cornbread stuffing mix

Direction

Brown the sausage in a large skillet and set aside to drain.

Put in the mushrooms and water. Bring to a boil before removing from the heat and stirring in the stuffing mix.

Allow it to sit for 5 minutes, covered.

7. Mushroom and Sausage Corn Bread Dressing

"A cornbread dressing made with a few of the most popular stuffing ingredients."

Serving: 9 cups

Preparation Time: 20 minutes

Ingredients

- 1½ cups yellow cornmeal
- 1/2 cup all-purpose flour
- 1 tsp. baking powder
- 1/2 tsp. baking soda
- 1/2 tsp. salt
- 1½ cups 2% milk
- 2 large eggs
- 1/4 cup plus 1 tbsp. olive oil, divided
- 1 tbsp. honey
- 1 tbsp. cider vinegar

Corn Bread Dressing:

- 1/2 lb. Jones No Sugar Pork Sausage Roll
- 8 oz. sliced fresh mushrooms
- 3 celery ribs, chopped
- 1 large onion, chopped
- 1½ cups soft whole wheat bread crumbs (3-4 slices)
- 3 large eggs, beaten
- 1 carton (32 oz.) of low-sodium chicken broth
- 1 tbsp. minced fresh rosemary
- 1 tsp. pepper

Direction

Preheat the oven to 425°F and place a 10-inch cast-iron skillet in it. Beat together the initial 5 ingredients.

Mix the vinegar, honey, 1/4 cup olive oil, eggs, and milk in a separate bowl. Beat the mixture into the dryer ingredients.

Transfer the skillet from the oven and lightly coat it with leftover olive oil.

Pour in the batter.

Let it bake for 15 minutes till golden brown. Allow it to cool for 10 minutes.

Transfer from the skillet to a cooling rack for baking and let it cool completely.

In the meantime, cook the sausage in a skillet over medium heat, crushing the meat until it is thoroughly cooked.

Take it out and set it aside to drain.

Cook the onion, celery, and mushrooms using the same skillet for approximately 5 minutes until the onion is soft.

Into a big bowl, crumble the cornbread, mix in mushroom mixture, sausage, and the rest of the ingredients.

Put the mixture into a 13x9-inch greased baking dish. Let it cool in the fridge for at least 8 hours with cover.

Remove from the refrigerator 30 minutes before baking.

Preheat the oven to 375°F.

Allow it to bake for 40 to 45 minutes or until browned and the mixture is set.

8. Chestnut, Apple and Sausage Corn Bread Dressing

"This cornbread recipe is loaded with vegetables, fruit, herbs, and turkey sausage."

Serving: 16

Preparation Time: 30 minutes

Ingredients

- 1 cup cornmeal
- 1 cup all-purpose flour
- 3 tsp. baking powder
- 1/4 cup sugar
- 1 tsp. salt
- 1/4 cup unsweetened applesauce
- 1 cup buttermilk
- 2 large egg whites

Dressing:

- 2 garlic cloves, minced
- 1 lb. turkey Italian sausage links, casings removed
- 2 medium tart apples, chopped
- 4 celery ribs, chopped
- 1 medium onion, chopped
- 3 tbsps. minced fresh parsley
- 1/2 tsp. dried thyme
- 1 medium sweet red pepper, chopped
- 1/2 tsp. pepper
- 1 cup chopped roasted chestnuts
- 1 cup reduced-sodium chicken broth
- 1 large egg white

Direction

To make the cornbread, combine the first 5 ingredients in a large mixing bowl.

Mix the egg whites, applesauce, and buttermilk in a mixing bowl. Stir the dry ingredients until moistened.

Place in an 8-inch square baking dish sprayed with cooking spray.

Allow it to bake for 20 to 25 minutes at 400°F.

When a toothpick inserted into the middle of the bake turns out completely clean, transfer it from the oven.

Allow it to cool on a cooking rack.

Cook the red pepper, onion, celery, and sausage in a large nonstick skillet over medium heat until the meat is no longer pink, and drain.

Place in a large mixing bowl.

On top of the mixture, crumble the cornbread.

Place the pepper, thyme, garlic, parsley, chestnuts, and apples in a mixing bowl.

Combine the egg white and broth.

Place in a 13x9-inch baking dish sprayed with cooking spray.

Cover with foil and bake at 325°F for 40 minutes.

Remove the cover and bake for another 10 minutes or until lightly browned.

9. Apple, Bacon, Sausage, And Cornbread Stuffing

"A delicious, moist cornbread stuffing recipe."

Serving: 12

Preparation Time: 30 minutes

Ingredients

- 8 oz. pork sausage links, finely chopped
- 1 (9x9 inch) pan of cornbread, cut into small cubes
- 1 lb. bulk pork sausage
- 1/2 lb. bacon slices, chopped
- 1 cup chopped celery
- 1 cup chopped onion
- 1 (16 oz.) package of mushrooms, sliced
- 1 cup chopped fresh parsley
- 2 Peeled, chopped, and cored Granny Smith apples
- 1 (14 oz.) package of dry bread stuffing mix
- 1 pinch salt and ground black pepper to taste
- 1 tbsp. dried sage leaves, or according to taste
- 2 (13.75 oz.) can chicken broth, or as needed

Direction

Preheat the oven to 175°C or 350°F. Lightly oil a baking dish, 9x13-inch in size.

Place the bread stuffing mix and cubed cornbread in a mixing bowl. Set it aside.

In a skillet, add ground sausage and chopped sausage links.

Cook and mix over medium-high heat till equally browned.

Allow it to drain before placing the sausage in a bowl.

Cook the bacon in the same skillet over medium heat until it turns brown.

Let the bacon drain on paper towels. Drain extra bacon fat from the skillet. Into the cornbread mixture, mix cooked bacon and sausage.

Cook the onion and celery for about 5 minutes with the same skillet over medium heat till soft and transparent. Mix into cornbread mixture.

Combine the apples, parsley, and mushrooms with the cornbread mixture.

Season with sage, pepper, and salt.

Toss the cornbread mixture with enough chicken broth to moisten it thoroughly. Spoon the mixture into the prepared baking dish.

Bake for 45 minutes in a preheated oven or until the center is firm and the top is toasted.

10. Savory Corn Bread Dressing

"A savory dressing baked alongside the turkey."

Serving: 12 servings (9 cups)

Preparation Time: 25 minutes

Ingredients

- 2½ cups chopped celery
- 1¼ cups chopped onions
- 10 tbsps. butter
- 7½ cups coarsely crumbled cornbread
- 2½ cups soft bread crumbs
- 4 tsp. rubbed sage
- 4 tsp. poultry seasoning
- 2 eggs, lightly beaten
- 1⅓ cups chicken broth

Direction

In a large skillet, sauté onions and celery with butter until soft. Transfer to a large mixing bowl.

Place the poultry seasoning, sage, bread crumbs, and cornbread in a mixing bowl.

Combine the broth and eggs. Add to the cornbread mixture and stir slowly to combine.

Place on a greased 2-quart baking plate.

Wrap with foil to cover and bake at 325°F for 30 minutes

Unwrap and bake for 10 minutes more until a thermometer reads 165°C and the stuffing turns lightly brown.

11. Shrimp Corn Bread Dressing

"A hearty delightful dressing."

Serving: 14

Preparation Time: 25 minutes

Ingredients

- 7 cups water divided
- 1 tbsp. seafood seasoning
- 1 lb. uncooked medium shrimp, peeled and deveined
- 1 large onion, chopped
- 1 celery rib, chopped
- 3 cups crumbled cornbread
- 1/2 cup chopped green pepper
- 3 green onions, chopped
- 1 package (14 oz.) of crushed seasoned stuffing or seasoned stuffing cubes
- 1 tsp. seasoned salt
- 1/8 tsp. garlic powder
- 1/2 cup butter, cubed
- 1/8 tsp. each of black, white, and cayenne pepper
- Celery leaves, optional

Direction

Pour 5 cups of water and the seafood seasoning to a boil in a large saucepan. Bring the shrimp back to a boil.

Reduce heat to low and leave to simmer for 2 minutes or until shrimp turns pink.

Allow to drain, and set aside 3 shrimp for garnish.

Slice the remaining shrimp.

In a skillet, sauté green onions, green pepper, celery, and onion with butter until soft.

In a mixing bowl, combine the seasonings, sautéed vegetables, chopped shrimp, cornbread, and stuffing.

Mix in the remaining water.

Place in a greased 13x9-inch baking dish.

Cover and bake at 350°F for 30 minutes.

Remove the cover and bake for 10 to 15 minutes or until lightly browned.

If desired, garnish with celery leaves and leftover shrimp.

12. Southern Cornbread Dressing

"A savory and simple chicken salad dressing recipe."

Serving: 18

Preparation Time: 1 hour 15 minutes

Ingredients

- 4 chicken breast halves, boneless and skinless
- 1 (1 lb.) a day-old loaf of white bread pulled into small pieces
- 4 tbsp. margarine
- 1 (16 oz.) package of dry cornbread mix
- 2 tsp. poultry seasoning
- 1/2 cup chopped onions
- 1/2 cup chopped celery
- 1 (10.75 oz.) can of condensed cream chicken soup
- 1/8 tsp. garlic powder
- 1/2 tsp. ground black pepper
- 6 eggs

Direction

Put the chicken breast in a saucepan and cover it with water. Bring the water to a rolling boil.

Allow for an hour of boiling time, or until the meat is soft and easily shredded.

Reserve the shredded chicken.

Set aside 4 to 6 cups of the remaining broth.

Follow the package directions to make an 8x8-inch pan of cornbread.

Crumble cornbread into a large mixing bowl.

Mix in the white bread.

Preheat the oven to 175 °C or 350 °F.

In a medium saucepan over medium heat, liquefy margarine and combine with celery and onions.

Cook gradually, stirring occasionally, until soft.

Combine the bread mixture with the celery and onions.

Mix the eggs, pepper, poultry seasoning, garlic powder, cream of chicken soup, 4 cups of the reserved broth, and the chicken.

Using a potato masher, mash the mixture until it has the consistency of gelatin.

Add more leftover broth as needed to achieve the desired consistency.

Place in a 9x13-inch baking dish.

Bake in a preheated oven for 30 minutes or until golden brown.

13. Southern Oyster Cornbread Dressing

"A great addition to your next thanksgiving dinner."

Serving: 4

Preparation Time: 45 minutes

Ingredients

- 2 eggs, beaten
- 1/4 cup butter
- 3 cups soft bread cubes
- 1/2 cup chopped parsley
- 1 pint drained in reserved liquid shucked oysters
- 4 green onions, chopped
- 1 red onion, chopped
- 2 stalks of celery, chopped
- 3 cups crumbled cornbread
- Salt and pepper

Direction

Preheat the oven to 175°C or 350°F.

Grease a 4-quart casserole dish.

Chop the oysters and sauté in 2 tablespoons of butter with celery, green onion, and red onion until soft.

In a large mixing bowl, combine 1/2 cup reserved oyster liquid, eggs, parsley, bread cubes, and cooked oyster and onion with cornbread.

Toss gently to combine; season with pepper and salt to taste.

Place dressing in a casserole dish and dot with remaining butter.

Bake uncovered for 45 minutes or until the top is golden brown.

14. Spicy Cranberry and Pecan Cornbread Stuffing

"Pecan, bacon, cranberries, and jalapenos in a cornbread."

Serving: 12

Preparation Time: 25 minutes

Ingredients

- 2 (14 oz.) packages of cornbread stuffing mix
- 1½ cups chicken stock
- 1/2 cup butter
- 1 cup white wine
- 2 cloves garlic, minced
- 10 slices bacon
- 1 small onion, chopped
- 1 cup chopped celery
- 1 (16 oz.) can of whole-berry cranberry sauce
- 1 (4 oz.) jar diced jalapeno peppers
- 1 (4 oz.) can of diced green chile peppers
- 1 cup chopped toasted pecans

Direction

Preheat the oven to 190°C or 375°F.

Place a large skillet over medium heat.

Cook the bacon in a skillet until crispy.

Place cooked bacon on a plate lined with paper towels to drain and cool and crumble the bacon.

Liquify butter in a large-sized skillet over medium-high heat.

Cook onion, garlic, and celery in hot butter till the onion begins to caramelize. Add wine to the skillet.

When the wine is warm, stir in the green chile peppers, jalapeno peppers, and cranberry sauce.

Allow the mixture to boil while covered.

Remove from heat and stir in the pecans and bacon.

Place stuffing mix in a large mixing bowl.

Mix the chicken stock and liquid mixture into the stuffing mix until it is thoroughly moist.

Place in a 9x13-inch baking dish.

Bake for 35 minutes in a preheated oven or until the top is brown.

15. Ultimate Cornbread Stuffing

"For a unique twist, top this bread with golden raisins, dried sweet cranberries, and toasted pecan pieces."

Serving: 8

Preparation Time: 20 minutes

Ingredients

- 2 (8.5 oz.) packages of corn muffin mix
- 2/3 cup heavy cream
- 2 eggs
- 2 tbsp. white sugar
- 2 tbsp. olive oil
- 1 tbsp. poppy seeds
- 1 tsp. vanilla extract
- 4 strips bacon, chopped
- 1 green bell pepper, chopped
- 1 red onion, chopped
- 1/4 tsp. dried marjoram
- 1½ cups chicken broth

Direction

Preheat the oven to 200 °C or 400 °F. Coat or oil a small square baking dish with cooking spray.

Combine the poppy seeds, vanilla, oil, sugar, eggs, cream, and muffin mix to create a batter.

Bake for 15 to 20 minutes until golden brown and the top springs back when lightly patted.

Allow it to cool completely before slicing it into small cubes and placing it in a bowl.

Reduce the oven temperature to 175 °C or 350 °F.

Brown the bacon in a large skillet over medium-high heat.

Cook and mix onions and peppers in a skillet until vegetables are soft.

Transfer from oven and place in a bowl with the cornbread squares. Add the chicken broth, season with marjoram, and stir well.

Cover with aluminum foil after spooning the mixture onto the baking dish.

Bake for 30 minutes or until thoroughly heated in a preheated oven.

16. Minute Microwave Cornbread

"This cornbread tastes better when baked in a conventional oven."

Serving: 6

Preparation Time: 7 minutes

Ingredients

- 1/2 cup all-purpose flour
- 2 tbsps. white sugar
- 1/2 cup cornmeal
- 2 tsp. baking powder
- 1/2 cup milk
- 1 egg
- 2 tbsp. vegetable oil
- 1/4 tsp. salt

Direction

Combine the vegetable oil, milk, egg, salt, baking powder, sugar, cornmeal, and flour in a microwave-safe glass or ceramic bowl.

Microwave on high for 3 minutes or until you use a toothpick to poke in the center of the bake, and it comes out clean.

If you don't have a rotating tray in your microwave, rotate the bowl halfway through cooking.

17. Absolute Mexican Cornbread

"The moistest and most delicious cornbread."

Serving: 6

Preparation Time: 15 minutes

Ingredients

- 1/2 cup shredded Cheddar cheese
- 4 eggs
- 1 cup white sugar
- 1 cup yellow cornmeal
- 1 (15 oz.) can of cream-style corn
- 1/2 (4 oz.) can of chopped green chile peppers, drained
- 1/2 cup Monterey Jack cheese, shredded
- 1 cup butter, melted
- 1 cup all-purpose flour
- 4 tsp. baking powder
- 1/4 tsp. salt

Direction

Preheat the oven to 150 °C or 300 °F.

Oil a 9x13-inch baking dish lightly.

In a large mixing bowl, combine the sugar and butter.

Whisk in the eggs one at a time.

Combine the Cheddar, Monterey Jack, chiles, and cream corn.

In a separate bowl, combine the salt, baking powder, cornmeal, and flour.

Mix the flour mixture into the corn mixture until smooth.

Place the batter in the prepared pan.

Bake for an hour in a preheated oven or until you use a toothpick to poke in the center of the bake and it comes out clean.

18. Amusement Park Cornbread

"A luscious cornbread with indescribably great flavor."

Serving: 8

Preparation Time: 10 minutes

Ingredients

- 2/3 cup white sugar
- 1 tsp. salt
- 1/3 cup butter, softened
- 1 tsp. vanilla extract
- 2 eggs
- 2 cups all-purpose flour
- 1 tbsp. baking powder
- 3/4 cup cornmeal
- 1⅓ cups milk

Direction

Preheat the oven to 200°C or 400°F.

Lightly oil an 8-inch skillet.

In a large mixing bowl, combine vanilla, butter, salt, and sugar until creamy.

Separate the eggs and whisk well after each addition.

Combine cornmeal, baking powder, and flour in a separate bowl.

Alternately add the flour mixture and milk to the egg mixture.

Whisk until thoroughly combined.

Bake for 20 minutes in a preheated oven until golden brown.

Serve while it's still warm.

19. Appalachian Corn Bread

"This cornbread is a great way to use the sweet type of corn."

Serving: 9

Preparation Time: 15 minutes

Ingredients

- 2 tbsp. chopped onion
- 4 tbsp. canola oil divided
- 1 cup all-purpose flour
- 2 tbsp. sugar
- 4 tsp. baking powder
- 2 large eggs
- 1/4 cup salsa
- 1 cup whole milk
- 1 cup cornmeal
- 1/2 tsp. salt
- 2 tbsp. minced chives
- 1/2 cup fresh or frozen corn, thawed
- 1/3 cup shredded cheddar cheese

Direction

Preheat the oven to 425°F.

In a small saucepan, sauté onion with 1 tablespoon of oil until soft. Set it aside.

In a large mixing bowl, combine the salt, baking powder, sugar, cornmeal, and flour.

Mix the milk, eggs, and the remaining oil in a separate bowl.

Incorporate the chives, salsa, cheese, corn, and reserved onion.

Mix into the dry ingredients until well combined.

Place in a greased 9-inch square baking pan.

Bake for 20 to 25 minutes or until you use a toothpick to poke in the center of the bake and it comes out clean.

Serve in squares while it's still warm.

20. Applesauce Cornbread

"A quick and easy cornbread recipe that goes great with chili, soup, or salad."

Serving: 9

Preparation Time: 10 minutes

Ingredients

- 1/2 tsp. salt
- 1 tsp. baking powder
- 1 cup fine cornmeal
- 1/4 cup sugar
- 1 cup all-purpose flour
- 3/4 cup skim milk
- 2 large eggs
- 2 tsp. baking soda
- 1/4 cup unsweetened applesauce

Direction

Preheat the oven to 220 °C or 425 °F.

Lightly grease an 8x8-inch baking pan.

Mix the sugar, baking powder, salt, baking soda, cornmeal, and flour in a mixing bowl.

In a separate bowl, combine the applesauce, eggs, and milk.

Fold the wet mixture into the dry mixture and thoroughly combine.

Then pour the combined mixture into the baking dish.

Bake in a preheated oven for 15 to 20 minutes or until brown and puffy.

21. Authentic Mexican Corn Bread

"A moist and sugary Mexican cornbread."

Serving: 12

Preparation Time: 15 minutes

Ingredients

- 2 tsp. vanilla extract
- 1/2 cup butter, melted
- 1 (15 oz.) can of cream-style corn
- 1 (14 oz.) can of sweetened condensed milk
- 2½ cups cornmeal
- 1/2 cup white sugar (optional)
- 1/2 cup all-purpose flour
- 5 large eggs
- 1 tbsp. baking soda
- 2 (15.25 oz.) cans whole kernel corn, drained and rinsed
- 1 tsp. salt

Direction

Preheat the oven to 175 °C or 350 °F.

Grease and flour a 2-quart baking plate.

In a mixing bowl, combine vanilla extract, eggs, sugar, and sweetened condensed milk.

Blend in the butter, cream-style corn, and whole-kernel corn.

Mix the salt, baking soda, flour, and cornmeal separately. Fold the cornmeal mixture into the corn mixture.

Pour the batter into the baking dish.

Bake for 45 minutes and poke the center with a toothpick.

Transfer it out from the oven when the toothpick comes out clean.

22. Avocado Cheese Cornbread

"A luscious avocado cheese bread."

Serving: 8

Preparation Time: 15 minutes

Ingredients

- 2 avocados – mashed, pitted and peeled.
- 2 eggs, beaten
- 1 cup shredded Monterey Jack cheese
- 1 (8 oz.) container of lemon-flavor yogurt
- 1 tbsp. fajita seasoning
- 1 cup self-rising cornmeal mix

Direction

Preheat the oven to 220°C or 425°F.

Grease a 9x13-inch baking pan.

Mix the fajita seasoning, cornmeal, cheese, yogurt, eggs, and avocados in a large mixing bowl.

Spread the mixture evenly in the oiled pan.

Bake for 17 minutes in a preheated oven or until the top is golden brown and a toothpick inserted into the center comes clean.

23. Bacon Cornbread

"A simple bread is spiced up with corn, cheese, and onion, then topped with bacon and poppy seeds."

Serving: 9

Preparation Time: 20 minutes

Ingredients

- 1 package (8½ oz.) cornbread muffin mix
- 1 large egg
- 1/2 cup frozen corn, thawed
- 1/3 cup whole milk
- 1/4 cup shredded cheddar cheese
- 1/4 cup grated onion
- 5 bacon strips, cooked and crumbled
- 1/2 tsp. poppy seeds, optional
- 1/8 tsp. paprika

Direction

In a mixing bowl, combine the first 6 ingredients.

Pour the batter into an 8-inch greased square baking pan.

Drizzle paprika and bacon over the top.

You can even sprinkle it with poppy seeds if you want.

Cook it in the oven for 20 to 25 minutes at 375°F.

Cut into pieces before serving.

24. Bacon Sweet Potato Cornbread

"A traditional and classic cornbread garnished with sweet potato and bacon."

Serving: 6

Preparation Time: 15 minutes

Ingredients

- 5 slices bacon
- 1¼ cups cornmeal
- 1 tsp. salt
- 1/2 tsp. baking soda
- 1 cup cooked sweet potato, mashed
- 1 cup buttermilk
- 2 eggs, lightly beaten

Direction

Preheat the oven to 230°C or 450°F.

Cook and mix the bacon in a 9-inch cast-iron skillet over medium-high heat for about 10 minutes or until browned.

Remove and cut the bacon, leaving a tablespoon of drippings in the skillet.

Mix the baking soda, salt, and cornmeal in a mixing bowl.

Thoroughly combine the eggs, buttermilk, and sweet potato in a separate bowl.

Mix the sweet potato mixture into the dry ingredients, then fold the chopped bacon.

Pour the batter into the cast-iron skillet.

Allow the cornbread to bake for about 30 minutes in a preheated oven or until it is firm to the touch and browned.

Transfer cornbread to a serving plate and cut it into wedges and serve.

25. Baked Bean Cornbread

"This moist bread recipe is so simple that even children can learn to bake it. It goes well with hotdogs and salads."

Serving: 6

Preparation Time: 15 minutes

Ingredients

- 2 packages (8½ oz. each) of cornbread muffin mix
- 2/3 cup milk
- 2 large eggs, lightly beaten
- 1 can (10 oz.) baked beans

Direction

In a large mixing bowl, combine the cornbread mixes, eggs, and milk.

Grease a 9-inch pie plate and pour one and a half cups of the batter.

Spread the remaining batter over the baked beans.

Allow it to bake for 25 to 30 minutes at 400°F without a cover.

Transfer it out of the oven when a toothpick inserted into the cornbread comes clean.

Serve while still warm.

26. Banana Cornbread

"This vegan-friendly recipe is delicious."

Serving: 24

Preparation Time: 10 minutes

Ingredients

- 2 cups all-purpose flour
- 2 cups cornmeal
- 2 cups milk
- 2 bananas
- 1⅓ cups white sugar
- 2/3 cup vegetable oil
- 7 tsp. baking powder
- 2 tsp. salt

Direction

Preheat the oven to 175°C or 350°F.

Grease a 9x13-inch baking dish.

In a mixing bowl, combine salt, baking powder, vegetable oil, sugar, banana, milk, cornmeal, and flour until smooth. Pour into a baking dish.

Bake for about 30 minutes in a preheated oven.

Transfer it out of the oven when a toothpick inserted into the cornbread comes clean.

27. Banana and Nut Cornbread

"This altered boxed cornbread mix is tasty with chopped walnuts and bananas. This recipe of fresh baked golden loaves is great to add to your brunch or bake sale."

Serving: 2 loaves (16 slices each)

Preparation Time: 10 minutes

Ingredients

- 2 packages (8½ oz. each) of cornbread muffin mix
- 1 cup mashed ripe bananas (about 2 medium size bananas)
- 1 cup chopped walnuts
- 1 cup 2% milk

Direction

In a large mixing bowl, mix all ingredients until combined.

Place in two greased 8 x 4-inch loaf pans.

Bake at 350°F for 35 to 45 minutes, poking the center with a toothpick.

Remove it from the oven when the toothpick comes out clean.

Allow it to cool for 10 minutes before removing it from the pans and transferring it to wire racks to cool completely.

28. Barbecued Cornbread Muffins

"This is a traditional cornbread recipe."

Serving: 1 dozen

Preparation Time: 20 minutes

Ingredients

- 1/2 lb. ground beef
- 1/4 cup packed brown sugar
- 1/4 cup ketchup
- 1 tbsp. Worcestershire sauce
- 1 tsp. prepared mustard
- 1/2 tsp. salt
- 1/4 tsp. pepper
- 1/4 tsp. garlic powder
- 1 package (8½ oz.) cornbread muffin mix
- 2/3 cup shredded cheddar cheese

Direction

Cook the beef in a large skillet over medium-high heat until it is no longer pink. Drain and place in a bowl.

Add the garlic powder, pepper, salt, mustard, Worcestershire sauce, ketchup, and brown sugar.

Prepare the cornbread mix according to the package directions.

Fill 2 tablespoons of batter into each oiled muffin cup.

Add the 2 tablespoons of beef mixture to each and sprinkle with cheese.

Put the remaining cornbread mix on top.

Bake for 12 to 15 minutes at 400°F1 and poke into the center with a toothpick.

Transfer it out from the oven when the toothpick comes out clean.

Allow it to cool for 5 minutes before transferring it to a cooking wire rack.

Serve warm, and keep the remaining in the fridge.

29. Basic Buttermilk Cornbread

"This recipe is for a southern classic."

Serving: 8

Preparation Time: 10 minutes

Ingredients

- 2 cups cornmeal
- 1½ cups buttermilk
- 1/4 cup vegetable oil
- 1 egg
- 2 tbsp. butter

Direction

Preheat the oven to 400°F or 200°C.

In a mixing bowl, combine the buttermilk, egg, cornmeal, and vegetable oil to make a batter.

Melt the butter in a cast-iron pan over medium heat, swirling to coat the sides and the bottom.

Heat the butter until it emits a faint toasted aroma, then add the batter to the hot pan.

Place the pan in a preheated oven and bake for 25-30 minutes or until golden brown.

30. Basic Cornbread Muffins

"A simple but luscious muffin recipe spiced up with jalapenos."

Serving: 12

Preparation Time: 10 minutes

Ingredients

- 1 cup cornmeal
- 1 cup all-purpose flour
- 2 tsp. baking powder
- 1/3 cup white sugar
- 1/2 tsp. salt
- 1/4 cup canola oil
- 1 egg, beaten
- 1 cup milk

Direction

Preheat the oven to 200 °C or 400°F.

Arrange the muffin pan with the baking paper liner or oil it.

In a large mixing bowl, combine salt, baking powder, sugar, flour, and cornmeal.

Mix in the milk, oil, and egg gradually.

Half-fill the muffin cups with batter.

Bake for 15 to 20 minutes, poking the center with a toothpick.

Remove it from the oven when the toothpick comes out clean.

31. Roasted Peppers and Monterey Jack Cornbread

"This basic cornbread can be dressed up with any of your favorite ingredients."

Serving: 12

Preparation Time: 25 minutes

Ingredients

- 1 tbsp. baking powder
- 1/2 cup unsalted butter, chilled and cubed
- 1/2 tsp. baking soda
- 1¼ cups all-purpose flour
- 1 cup chopped onion
- 1¾ cups cornmeal
- 1/4 cup white sugar
- 1½ tsp. salt
- 1½ cups buttermilk
- 3 eggs
- 1½ cups shredded pepper jack cheese
- 2 oz. drained and chopped roasted marinated red bell peppers
- 1⅓ cups thawed and drained frozen corn kernels
- 1/2 cup chopped fresh basil

Direction

Preheat the oven to 205 °C or 400 °F. Butter a 9x9x2 inch baking pan.

Liquefy 1 tablespoon of butter over medium-low heat in a nonstick skillet.

Add the onion and sauté for 10 minutes till soft. Let it cool.

Mix the baking soda, cornmeal, salt, baking powder, sugar, and flour in a mixing bowl.

Add 7 tablespoons of butter, and massage with your fingertips until the mixture resembles a coarse meal.

In a mixing bowl, blend the buttermilk and eggs.

Pour the mixture into the dry ingredients and swirl until incorporated.

Mix in the onion, basil, red peppers, corn, and cheese.

Add to the prepared pan.

Allow the cornbread to bake for 45 minutes, and poke the center with a toothpick.

Transfer it out from the oven when the toothpick comes out clean.

Allow it to cool in the pan for 20 minutes. Cut the cornbread into squares.

32. Batter Cornbread

"A classic corn meal pancake cornbread."

Serving: 10

Preparation Time: 10 minutes

Ingredients

- 1 cup buttermilk
- 2/3 cup cornmeal
- 1 egg, slightly beaten
- 3 tbsp. butter, melted
- 3/4 tsp. salt
- 1/2 tsp. baking soda
- cooking spray

Direction

In a mixing bowl, combine the baking soda, salt, butter, egg, cornmeal, and buttermilk until blended.

Preheat a large skillet or griddle over medium heat.

Coat the pan with nonstick cooking spray. Drop heaping tablespoons onto the griddle.

Allow it to cook for 2 to 3 minutes or until bubbles form on top.

Turn and brown the other side for another 2 to 3 minutes.

33. Blueberry Cornbread Muffins

"Tender and moist corn muffins with blueberries!"

Serving: 12

Preparation Time: 15 minutes

Ingredients

- 1¼ cups all-purpose flour
- 1 cup yellow cornmeal
- 1/2 cup white sugar
- 1/2 tsp. salt
- 2 tsp. baking powder
- 1 tsp. baking soda
- 1/4 cup vegetable oil
- 2½ tsp. vanilla extract
- 1 egg
- 1 cup buttermilk
- 1½ cups fresh blueberries

Direction

Preheat the oven to 200°C or 400°F.

Line the muffin cups with paper liners or grease them.

In a large mixing bowl, combine baking soda, baking powder, salt, sugar, cornmeal, and flour.

In a separate bowl, combine the egg, vanilla, and oil.

Alternately, use buttermilk to moisten the egg mixture in the dry ingredients.

Gently fold in the blueberries.

Fill the muffin cups halfway with the batter.

Bake until golden for 20-25 minutes in a preheated oven, then serve warm.

34. The Best Cornbread Muffins

"Very easy to make, and the ingredients are convenient to find."

Serving: 12

Preparation Time: 8 minutes

Ingredients

- 1/4 cup butter, softened
- 9 tbsp. white sugar
- 2 eggs
- 1 tbsp. vanilla extract
- 1½ cups biscuit baking mix
- 1/4 cup yellow cornmeal
- 2/3 cup milk

Direction

Cream the sugar and butter in a large mixing bowl until fluffy and light.

Mix in the eggs one at a time, whisking thoroughly after each addition, and then add the vanilla extract.

In a separate bowl, combine the cornmeal and baking mix.

Mix this into the butter/egg mixture, alternately with the milk, until well combined.

Fill the muffin cups halfway with the batter.

In a preheated oven, bake for 20 to 30 minutes or until golden.

Conclusion

Thank you for joining us on our journey through the delicious world of cornbread.

We hope you've learned something new and are now confident in your ability to prepare a variety of cornbreads recipe!

Remember, the more you bake bread, the better you'll become.

So, get your hands dirty without further ado and bake some cornbread!

If you're a big fan of cornbread, you're a big foodie, and we salute you!

Try these delectable recipes and make your family smile!

About the Author

Owen isn't your typical cookbook writer. He built a life and career as a successful stockbroker in New York for many years, getting into the routine of it all. He enjoyed the crazy schedule, his exploding inbox, and endless phone conversations with clients. Still, he always found himself in the kitchen when he had some time to spare. Even if he got home at 11:00 pm and had an early morning meeting the next day, he always cooked delicious meals and dinners for himself.

When the pandemic hit and lots of his clients started pulling out, Owen began to question whether he would even have a job within the next couple of months. Once the world went into lockdown, his job became harder with the sudden obstacles of working from home with a job like his. His stress, however, was very fruitful because it often resulted in new dishes.

More than a home office, at one point, his place felt more like a restaurant. Whether it was breakfast, lunch, or dinner, he was always whipping up something amazing! When he was let go, he was relieved to finally have more time to work on new recipes to share with his friends and family. Eventually, they encouraged him to start writing cookbooks… and that's how he began his new life as an amateur cook and cookbook writer. Now, he travels across the US searching for inspiration for his recipes, but he always finds his way back home to his cozy townhouse in New Jersey, ready to share all of his new dishes with his loved ones.

Appendices

Thank you ♥

Hey, guys! I just wanted to say thanks for supporting me by purchasing one of my e-books. I have to say—when I first started writing cookbooks, I didn't have many expectations for myself because it was never a part of "the plan." It was more of a hobby, something I did for me and decided to put out there if someone might click on my book and buy it because they liked my food. Well, let me just say it's been a while since those days, and it's been a wild journey!

Now, cookbook writing is a huge part of my life, and I'm doing things I love! So, THANK YOU for trusting me with your weekly meal preps, weekend BBQs, 10-minute dinners, and all of your special occasions. If it weren't for you, I wouldn't be able to concentrate on producing all sorts of delicious recipes, which is why I've decided to reach out and ask for your help. What kind of recipes would you like to see more of? Are you interested in special diets, foods made with kitchen appliances, or just easy recipes on a time-crunch? Your input will help me create books you want to read with recipes you'll actually make! Make sure to let me know, and your suggestions could trigger an idea for my next book…

Take care!

Owen

Printed in Great Britain
by Amazon

530f5750-fa71-4849-8f74-e2f564286764R01